Rookie
Read-About® Math

Farmer's Market Rounding

By Julie Dalton

Subject Consultant
Robyn Silbey
Math Content Coach
Montgomery County Public Schools
Maryland

Reading Consultant
Cecilia Minden-Cupp, PhD
Former Director, Language and Literacy Program
Harvard Graduate School of Education

Children's Press®
A Division of Scholastic Inc.
New York   Toronto   London   Auckland   Sydney
Mexico City   New Delhi   Hong Kong
Danbury, Connecticut

Special thanks to Sigona's Farmer's Market for the use
of their location and their cooperation in the
shooting of photographs for this book.

Designer: Herman Adler Design
The photo on the cover shows Miguel and his father at the farmer's market.

Library of Congress Cataloging-in-Publication Data

Dalton, Julie, 1951–
    Farmer's market rounding / by Julie Dalton.
        p. cm. — (Rookie read-about math)
    Includes index.
    ISBN10: 0-516-25424-3 (lib. bdg.)   0-516-25551-7 (pbk.)
    ISBN13: 978-0-516-25424-1 (lib. bdg.)   978-0-516-25551-4 (pbk.)
    1. Arithmetic—Juvenile literature. 2. Estimation theory—Juvenile literature.
I. Title. II. Series.
    QA115.D35 2006
    513—dc22

                                                            2005032730

Miguel and his dad are going to the farmer's market. They want to buy tomatoes, onions, and hot peppers.

Miguel's dad carries
a basket, and Miguel
carries a pad of paper
and a pencil. Miguel will
keep track of how much
money they spend.

6

Miguel's dad will choose
the food and put it into
the basket. He will tell
Miguel how much it costs.
Then Miguel will round
the cost to the nearest ten.

Miguel knows rounded
numbers are easier to add.
He tells his dad a rhyme
he learned at school
about rounding.

If a number ends with 4, 3, 2, or 1,

Rounding down should be done.

If a number ends with 6, 7, 8, or 9,

Then rounding up will be just fine.

Numbers ending with 5 are halfway there.

So round them up without a care.

10

Miguel's father chooses two tomatoes and puts them into the basket. He tells Miguel that each tomato costs 68¢.

Miguel thinks: A tomato costs 68¢. Sixty-eight has eight ones, so he must round **up** to the nearest ten. Since sixty-eight has six tens, he rounds up to seventy.

Miguel writes 70¢ on the paper two times, once for each tomato.

14

Next, Miguel's dad chooses two onions and puts them into the basket. He tells Miguel that each onion costs 33¢.

Miguel thinks: The onions cost 33¢ each. Thirty-three has three ones, so he must round **down** to the nearest ten. Miguel writes 30¢ on the paper two times, once for each onion.

70¢
70¢
30¢
30¢

18

Miguel's dad then chooses three hot peppers and puts them into the basket. He tells Miguel that each pepper costs 15¢.

Miguel thinks: The hot peppers cost 15¢ each. Fifteen has five ones, so he must round **up** to the nearest ten. Miguel writes 20¢ on the paper three times, once for each hot pepper.

Miguel and his dad finished shopping. They looked at the paper with the rounded numbers written on it:

70¢
70¢
30¢
30¢
20¢
20¢
20¢

Miguel's dad helps Miguel add the numbers on the paper. They find that it cost them about $2.60 to buy the tomatoes, onions, and hot peppers.

25

Miguel and his dad go back home. They chop the onions, tomatoes, and hot peppers to make a snack called salsa. Miguel loves to eat chips and salsa.

Miguel likes to help his dad shop. He also likes to help his dad keep track of what they spend. Rounding is a good skill to know.

Miguel is glad his dad helped him practice. Now it's time to eat!

Words You Know

basket

farmer's market

hot peppers

onions

rounding

salsa

tomatoes

31

Index

About the Author

Julie Dalton is an editor and writer who lives in central Connecticut with a big dog, a gentle cat, and several teenagers.

Photo Credits